Paul Arsenault, O.M.I.

The History of Notre-Dame du Cap

Éditions Notre-Dame du Cap

Front cover photo : Claude Guillemette
Back cover photo : Richard Normandin

Les Éditions Notre-Dame du Cap
622, Notre-Dame
Cap-de-la-Madeleine, Québec
G8T 4G9

Legal deposit : 1st quarter 1988
National Library of Canada
National Library of Québec
ISBN : 2-921012-01-4

Preface

Our Lady welcomes you!

Welcome to Notre-Dame du Cap National Shrine, one of those exceptional halts still to be found along the highway of modern life.

Join in the hymns of praise which rise towards Mary from this earthly haven, as they have risen since the first establishment of the Jesuits in 1651. Join the procession of pilgrims who have made their way in an unceasing flow to the Little Shrine, since its dedication to Our Lady in 1888.

Join us on the spreading acres of the Shrine, which constant tending over the years have turned into an oasis of green, of trees and flowers, where Nature, at Our Lady's bidding, welcomes her children in beauty and calm, in silence and meditation.

In these surroundings, you may well hear Mary urging you to pursue your pilgrimage into the very depths of your heart, where she will bring you into the presence of her Son and teach you to hear His words: "Come unto me, all of you who are tired from carrying heavy loads, and I will give you rest" (Mat. 11:28).

If you heed His words, the heaviest of crosses will become bearable, the stoniest of hearts will melt, your surfeit of sin will find pardon, the mists that shroud the pathway of your life will dissolve into sunlight. In the words of Our Holy Father, the Pope: here you may experience "hours of heaven".

The Oblates of Mary Immaculate take pleasure in welcoming you in the name of Our Lady. It is a privilege we have enjoyed since May 2, 1902 which explains why I have the honour of welcoming you here. And also why the Oblates devote more and more of their time and energy to celebrating through their words, through their writings and through their chants, the wonders accomplished by Mary in this Shrine of Cap de la Madeleine.

Father Paul Arsenault is one of this number and it is he who will guide us through this historic album.

During the score of years he has passed at the Shrine he has discovered many secrets and has spent much time meditating on its mysteries.

When you read through this album and when you accomplish your pilgrimage, you will realize that the Oblates are not alone in their "home mission", the Shrine. There are many who collaborate in this work, many are ordained members of the church, but it is above all the lay workers who share with us the responsibility of the Shrine and help with its social organization.

And so together, united in our hearts, we bid you belcome to the National Shrine of Notre-Dame du Cap.

Welcome to the house of Our Lady!

Marcel Zago, O.M.I.
Superior General

Rome, February 17, 1988

Introduction

With what words can we describe this place of pilgrimage? The Shrine of Notre-Dame du Cap may be compared to a spring whose waters have welled up for over three centuries. It may be likened to a tree planted at the water's edge: its branches bear fruit in due season and its leaves never wither. Or, again, it resembles the seed cast into the ground which, nurtured with the blood of martyrs, yielded its crop a hundredfold.

One cannot write the history of Notre-Dame du Cap and make no mention of Faith. This century-old work of man is rooted in Faith and commitment to God. For this reason, the present album is not presented as a history book, nor yet as a story book. It is intended as a description of acts and actors illuminated by Faith and by the Word of God. It is written as a reminder to our hearts of a holy chronicle: the story of the mediation of God and Mary, a mediation which, over the centuries, has created the Shrine of Notre-Dame du Cap and set it apart in its own image.

We adopt for our own the reminder made by Pope Jean-Paul II to the rectors of shrines: "The traditional and ever-flourishing vocation of sanctuaries is to act as an aerial which ceaselessly captures the Good News of Salvation". But why come so far to hear the Word of God? Why come so far in order to pray? It is our belief that certain places speak more intimately to our hearts. For example, the place where we spent a happy childhood; the place where we encountered the love of our lifetime; the place where precious hours were spent. We are drawn to such places and from time to time we wish to return to them. Such places warm our hearts. They possess a soul. They have a past. The Shrine of Notre-Dame du Cap is no exception to this rule.

Paul Arsenault, O.M.I.

"A sandy mound
of no use
to man or beast"

The unanimous testimony of generations of pilgrims confirms the parable of the sower who went into the fields to sow. Here, as in the Gospel, the seeds fell on all sorts of ground. In the early days of the colonies, the sceptics dismissed Cap de la Madeleine as "a sandy mound of no use to man or beast." Events since then would probably surprise them. God sowed their sandy mound and it became fertile and its yield has been abundant.

Since the middle of the seventeenth century, when the first missionary came through, millions of pilgrims have made a special journey to bring greetings to their Mother. They make their special journey... to a sandy mound! More than half a century ago a writer was already noting that "The National Shrine of the Virgin in Cap de la Madeleine is visited by thousands of pilgrims each year. They come from all over to ask for blessings, to find ease of heart, to sing their gratitude."

Four generations brought together. In the foreground, the 1714 shrine; to the left, the former church of Saint Madeleine; to the right, the 1904 extension; in the background, the bell-tower of the basilica under construction.

1885

One of the first pilgrimages to Notre-Dame du Cap.

1915

Pilgrims gathered in front of the Shrine and the 1904 extension.

1950

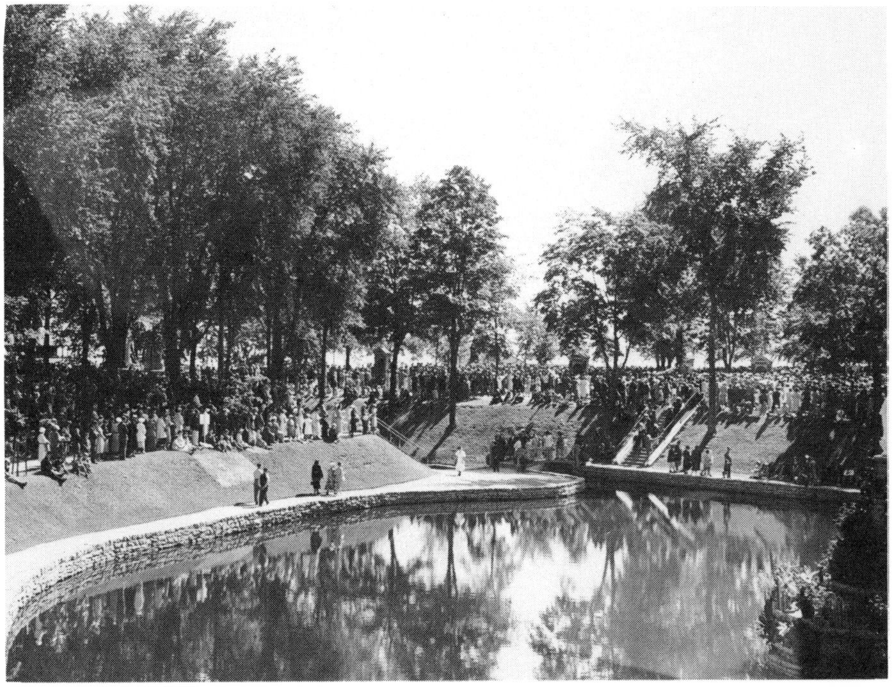

Pilgrims in prayer as they process through the gardens of the Virgin by lake Sainte-Marie.

1978

Pilgrimage of Québec seniors outside the basilica after the sacrament of the Eucharist.

1980

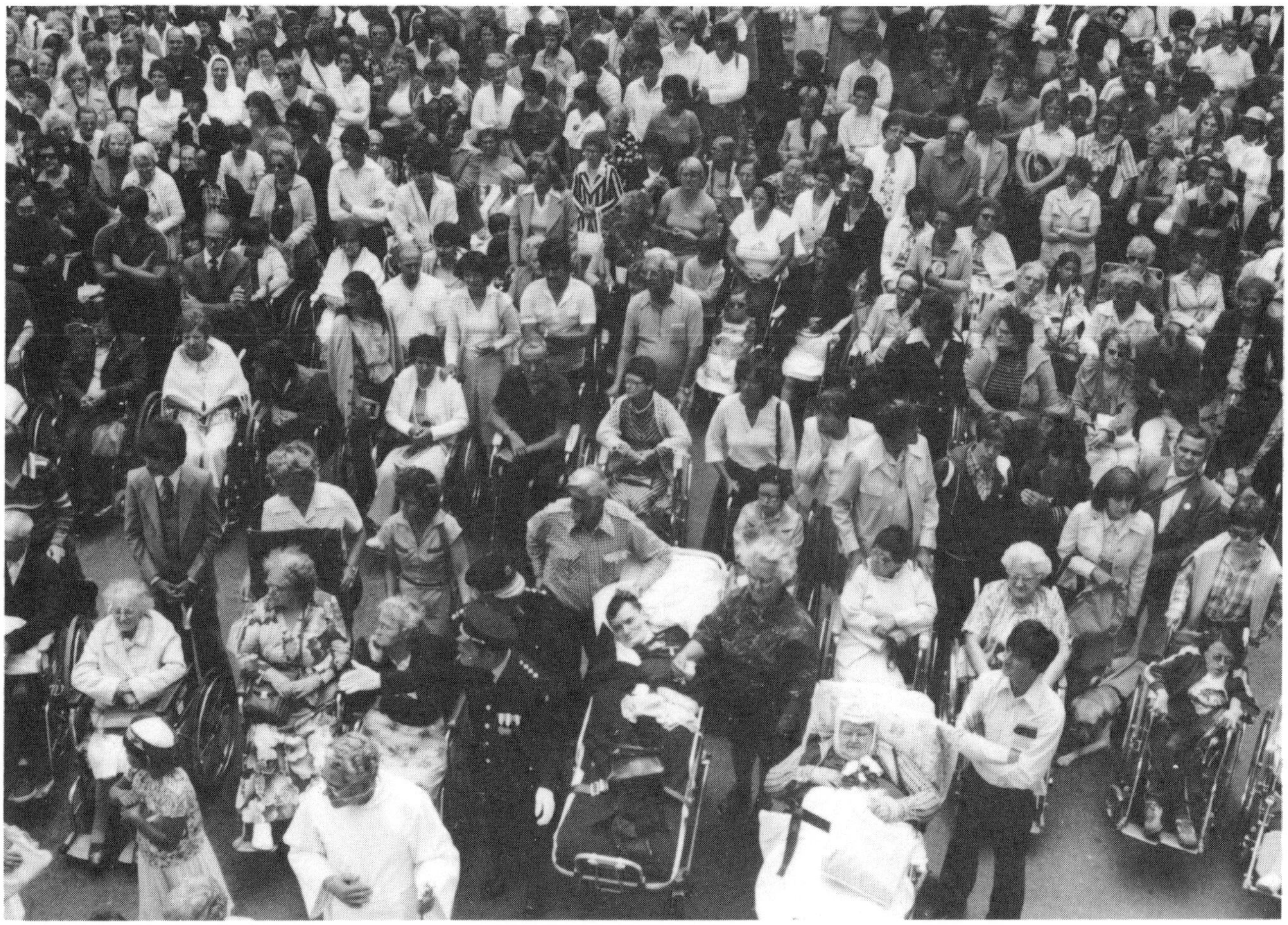

Pilgrimage of the sick and handicapped on the Feast of the Assumption.

We of today's world are part of the living stream of faith and tenacity that has flowed down from those that came before. We welcome the words of Peter's successor when he says: "Today, indeed, we come to Notre-Dame du Cap as people of our time. We come to renew with those past generations with whom we share our faith in the Mother of God. A fine inheritance has been bequeathed to you. It has made you what you are. And the cornerstone of that inheritance is faith, and underpinning that faith is devotion to Mary, to which your predecessors dedicated themselves.. We are here to, as it were, transfer this sharing of faith into the hearts of our generation and their successors."

Those generations of early witnesses provide us, who are here, with our inspiration. Intrepid as the prophets, they generated faith, fanned it into flame, tended it lest it die out in the ashes of scepticism. When we are tempted to loosen our grasp on hope, it is their faith in the future which upholds and stimulates us. Through the generations it is the pilgrims' faith that confirms the special vocation of this Shrine.

"Born
through suffering..."

"With our own ears we have heard it, O God -- our ancestors have told us about it, about the great things you did in their time, in the days of long ago..."

Psalm 44

The coming of a child is always preceded by lengthy preparations and a time of waiting. The long-desired birth has its own history of events, places and people. So it was with the Shrine of Notre-Dame du Cap. It was not created through chance, nor through spontaneous generation. It was no test-tube baby. It was conceived as any child may be conceived, by men and women who worked with God to bring this "son of man" into the world. The birth was the living witness to Faith in a part of the country which has never lacked for witnesses or prophets.

One of its first pastors gave a very cogent account of this heaven-inspired labour when he said: "This work bears God's stamp all the more clearly because it was born through suffering." No creation of great scale is possible if one is not willing to pay the price. And that price was dearly paid by those pioneers who created this place of pilgrimage. "Those who wept as they went out carrying the seed will come back singing for joy as they bring in the harvest." Nothing worthwhile can ever be achieved without taking time and pains.

In the middle of the 17th century, Québec was a French colony; Cap de la Madeleine a sparsely inhabited township. Our story really began with the appearance of Jacques de La Ferté, a Frenchman and priest of Sainte-Marie-Madeleine, in Chateaudun. In exchange for a compensatory award from the Company of New France, he made over to the Jesuits a domain to be used for evangelizing the local inhabitants. The deed, dated March 20, 1651, describes: "a fief and domain ten leagues wide, situated along the great St. Lawrence river and stretching twenty leagues inland."

On September 8, 1634, Cap de la Madeleine received its first missionary, Jacques Buteux, a Jesuit, accompanied by Father Paul Lejeune. As predicant of the St. Maurice region, Father Buteux helped the first settlers by granting them land to clear and sow. There were at that time fourteen settlers in Cap de la Madeleine. One of a number of Jesuit pioneers in the area, Jacques Buteux, was martyred by the Iroquois on May 10, 1652. The Jesuits spent 25 years in Cap de la Madeleine and were succeeded by the Recollet order towards 1680. Amongst the first families to settle in the budding village we find names such as Houdan, Boivin, Houssart, Guillet, Pépin, Beaudry, Aubuchon, Fafard, Boucher, etc.

In 1659, the Jesuits granted Sir Pierre Boucher a domain, lying within their property at Cap de la Madeleine. He called his estate "fief Sainte-Marie" and built the first chapel, which was moved in 1662 onto the land now belonging to the Shrine. This chapel became the first church in Cap de la Madeleine, the Church of Sainte-Marie-Madeleine. We can still see remains of that first church, embedded in the walls of the present-day Shrine. Without being aware of it, Pierre Boucher, former Governor of Trois-Rivières, was the first artisan of the Shrine of Notre-Dame du Cap.

This miniature chapel, a gift to the Historical Society of Cap de la Madeleine, was erected on the side of Highway 138 on October 27, 1940. At the end of the summer of 1982, it was moved to the frontage of Cap de la Madeleine cemetery.

In Nomine Sanctissimæ Trinitatis, Patris & Filij, & Spiritus Sancti, & ad laudem, & gloriam Beatissimæ Dei Genitricis Virginis Mariæ D. N. piamque venerationem D. P. N. Dominici SS. Rosarij auctoris, atque institutoris.

Fr. Antoninus Cloche Sacræ Theologiæ Professor, Ordinis Prædicatorum humilis Magister Generalis, & Seruus. Omnibus præsentes litteras inspecturis salutem in Domino sempiternam.

QVEMADMODVM Christianæ perfectionis summam in vnit[illegible] fidelium ad Christum, veluti membrorum ad caput, omnium perfectionum fontem, necnon vnione Christianorum ad inuicem consistere credimus, ita ad illam adipiscendam optimum esse orationi[illegible] medium, ratione, & experientia piè edocemur; Modus verò Deum orandi, secundùm quem Sanctissima Virgo MARIA Mater DEI per centum quinquaginta Salutationes Angelicas, & quindecim D[illegible]ominicas Orationes instar Dauidici Psalterij colitur, qui ROSARIVM nuncupatur, à Sanctissimo Patre Nostro DOMINICO primùm inuentus, & institutus, à Summis Romanis Pontificibus [illegible] ad deuotam Patrum Nostri Ordinis intercessionem approbatus, priuilegijs quoque maximis, ac innumeris Indulgentijs, alijsque Apostolicis gratijs decoratus, inter cœteros in Ecclesia inuentos ad [illegible] obtinendum (vt piè credimus) magnoperè confert, nam præter hoc quòd Beatissima Dei Genitrix, cuius intercessio nobis perfectionem hanc impetrare potest ibi crebriùs inuocatur, ipse quoque per [illegible] modus orandi [illegible] quàm facillimè compendio illam consequitur, dum IESV CHRISTI Saluatoris Nostri vitam omnem per quindecim Mysteria digestam meditando percurrere faci[illegible]. Quæ Vos in Christo d[illegible]ectissimi, & deuotissimi Christi fideles loci [illegible] piè considerantes, ad habendum, augendum, & conseruandum prædictum modum orandi, Confraternitatem Psalterij, seu ROSARII sub inuocatione Beatæ MARIÆ Virginis in Ecclesia [illegible] dicti loci instituendi, & ordinandi, eiusque Altare, & Cappellam fundandi & erigendi à Nobis insta[illegible]ntissimè petiuistis per interpositam personam Vobis licentiam impartiri cum gratijs, & fauoribus opportunis; Nos igitur vestris votis, & pijs petitionibus inclinati, dictam Confraternitatem sic vt præfertur, instituendi auctoritate Apostolica Nobis concessa, tenore præsentium licentiam concedimus, & facultatem, accedente tamen assensu Ordinarij loci, ac Prioris vicinioris Conuentus, seu loci Ordinis nostri, ac media prædicatione alicuius Patris [illegible] nostri per suum Superiorem destinandi. Vtriusque sexus Christifideles in eam recipiendos cum gratijs, & Indulgentijs sibi à Romanis Pontificibus concessis, prout aliæ consimiles Confraternitates in Ecclesijs nostri Ordinis [illegible] recipimus, & admittimus in vita pariter, & in morte. Admonentes eiusdem Sanctissimi ROSARII festum prima Dominica mensis Octobris singulis annis in eadem Cappella celebrari debere, iuxta [illegible] recordationis GREGORII XIII. decretum, & institutum in gratiarum actionem præteritæ, & memorandæ victoriæ contra Turcas eiusdem [illegible] Societatis Confratrum fusis precibus eadem die (vt piè credimus) ac auxilio, & interuentu eiusdem Beatissimæ Virginis MARIÆ Dominæ nostræ impetratæ, atque obtentæ. Cuius Societatis, & Cappellæ Cappellanum deputamus [illegible] qui nomina, & cognomina omnium Christifidelium in eandem Societatem ingredi, & deuotè recipi petentium [illegible] ad hoc specialiter deputat[illegible] possit scribere, Psalteria, seu Coronas benedicere, Sacri ROSARII Mysteria frequenter exponere, ac omnia, & singula facere, quæ Fratres nostri in Ecclesijs nostris ad hoc deputati facere possunt, & ritè consueuerunt, in diem Christi eiusdem conscientiam onerantes, ne pro huiusmodi admissione, ingressu, scriptura, & benedictione aliquid omninò temporalis lucri quomodolibet exigat, sed gratis hæc omnia præstet quemadmodum ipsius piæ Societatis Capitula habent, & sanctiones, vti etiam Nos in Dei cultum, eiusque Sanctissimæ Matris gloriam, & Christifidelium salutem, & profectum gratis accepimus, & gratis damus, & concedimus. Volumus autem, & omninò obseruari iubemus, quod in Ven. Icone dictæ Cappellæ quindecim nostræ redemptionis Sacra Mysteria pingantur, necnon pro huiusce concessionis [illegible] consentanea recognitione in eadem Icone Diui Patris nostri DOMINICI eiusdem ROSARII primarij Auctoris Imago Veneranda flexis genibus de manu Deiparæ Virginis Coronas orarias accipientis similiter pingatur, notumque facimus, PAVLVM PAPAM V. felicis recordationis per suum Breue datum Romæ apud S. Marcum die vigesima Septembris M. DC. VIII. restituisse Societati Sacratissimi ROSARII confirmassèque omnes Indulgentias concessas eidem à Summis Pontificibus Romanis Prædecessoribus suis, quibus hactenus dicta Societas fruebatur, ac si litteræ reuocationis earundem non emanassent; sicut etiam INNOCENTIVM XI. in suo Breui Dat. Romæ apud Sanctam Mariam Maiorem sub Annulo Piscatoris die 31. Iulij anno 1679. gratias, & priuilegia non auxisse solùm, sed etiam omnium indulgentiarum summarium eidem Breui inscruisse. Decernimus insuper, & declaramus postremò, quòd quandocumque contigerit dictos Fratres Nostros ibidem Ecclesiam obtinere, ipso iure, ipsoque facto ex nunc pro tunc, absque alia declaratione, sed præsentium tenore dictam Societatem, ac omnes Indulgentias, & priuilegia eidem concessa ablata esse à dicta Cappella, & penitùs atque totaliter ad dictam nostram Ecclesiam translata cum omnibus bonis temporalibus dictæ Societati quomodolibet acquisitis. Quam conditionem Superiores, & Officiales tàm Ecclesiæ prædictæ, quàm Confraternitatis admittere, & manu propria subscribere teneantur. Quæ omnia in Instrumento publico manu Notarij faciendo poni debent, & explicari. In nomine Patris, & Filij, & Spiritus Sancti Amen. Quibuscumque in contrarium non obstantibus. In quorum fidem his Patentibus litteris officij nostri sigillo munitis manu propria subscripsimus gratis, vbique, & semper. Datum Romæ xj Maij 1694.

Fr. Antoninus Cloche

Magister Ordinis.

R.^{ta} fol. 280

Fr. Antoninus Massoulie Requisitor Ordinis [illegible]

The Latin text of the Charter of the Brotherhood of the Rosary, dated May 11, 1694.

The former Jesuit manor, in the early days of Cap de la Madeleine. A second manor was built on this site in 1742 (today 555, Notre-Dame Street).

By the end of the seventeenth century those first pioneer seedings were already promising a harvest. Following the ministry of the itinerant missionaries, Cap de la Madeleine welcomed its first resident parish priest, Paul Vachon. Born in Beauport on November 8, 1656, Father Vachon was ordained on December 21, 1680 by Monsignor de Laval in the basilica of Québec. When he was appointed to Cap de la Madeleine on October 14, 1685, Father Vachon was given only the status of non-resident priest. On September 18, 1694, Monsignor de Saint Vallier appointed him resident priest. It was Paul Vachon who began the devotion to the Rosary in Cap de la Madeleine. On May 11, 1694, he obtained an official certificate from Rome, allowing him to set up one of the first Brotherhoods of the Rosary in Canada. This prophetic action stimulated a wave of Marian devotion in the St. Maurice region.

The first church in Cap de la Madeleine included a Brotherhood chapel in which Father Vachon set up a statue of the Virgin in silver circa 1725. Today, we do not know what happened to that first statue of Mary. Father Vachon's dream was to build a church which would be larger than Pierre Boucher's simple chapel, then more than fifty years old and more than a little tumble-down. In spite of the fact that his parish was both small and poor (in 1721 there were but 16 households of which eleven only paid tithes) Father Vachon, subsequent to the issue of a decree by Monsignor de Saint Vallier, soon began the construction of a stone church. Father Vachon died on March 7, 1729, forty-four years after his arrival in Cap de la Madeleine. The accomplishments of his productive ministry have stood the test of time.

In those days, most houses had a small private chapel dedicated to Mary, to whom were ascribed a great variety of attributes: Our Lady of Joy; Our Lady of Present Help; Our Lady of Victory; Our Lady of Compassion. The chapel was a gathering place in the evening for the Family Rosary.

Je me souviens

I shall not forget

1608 : Champlain founded Québec City.
1634 : Laviolette founded Trois-Rivières.
1642 : Maisonneuve founded Ville-Marie (Montréal).
1659 : Monsignor de Laval arrived in Québec City on June 16 to take up his post as vicar apostolic of New France.
1660 : France's Golden Age under Louis XIV, known as the Sun-King.
1663 : Louis XIV incorporated New France into the Royal domain.
1674 : Monsignor de Laval was appointed Bishop of Québec City on October 1. He remained in that post till 1688.
1678 : Foundation of the parish of Sainte Marie Madeleine du Cap by Monsignor de Laval, on October 30.
1689 : The Lachine Massacre.
1690 : The British seized Acadia and Newfoundland.

Contemporary writers at this epoch included Corneille, Racine, Molière, Pascal, Lafontaine, Boileau, Bossuet and Fénelon.

"Look kindly down where by the mighty river
A stripling nation grows in ardent adoration
Consoled by Thee so often in its trials,
Defended oft by Thy most powerful arm."

Free translation of "Notre-Dame du Canada", E. Desjardins, S.J.

"For the Honour of the Great Saint"

Painting by LeBlond, 1720. Original on the left-hand wall of the Shrine.

"...at the end of our sermon, we declared to the habitants that we intended they should manifest their ardour by working on the construction of a new church, and we have promised an abundant contribution towards the fabric... and we do so exhort them for the honour of the great Saint, their patron..."

Monsignor de Saint-Vallier, May 13, 1714.

Up till then, there had been nothing to indicate that Cap de la Madeleine was destined to a special vocation. Here, as elsewhere, missionaries had come, stayed a while, then passed on, leaving the evangelical message. The parish of Sainte Marie Madeleine, established on October 30, 1678 by Monsignor de Laval began to organize itself. Monsignor de Laval's successor, Monsignor de Saint Vallier, during a pastoral visit to Cap de la Madeleine on May 13, 1714, signed the decree authorizing construction of a new parish church.

Resources were limited and there was very little building stone to be found in the immediate area. So, in 1716, Father Vachon organized a region-wide fund-raising drive. Work on the new church began only in the summer of 1717. Volunteer workers cleared the site, dug the foundations and transported the building materials. The unpretentious church of St. Madeleine began to rise, thanks to these unpaid helpers searching out suitable stones here and there in the surrounding fields and struggling back with them to the building site. On June 17, 1717, the cornerstone was laid. The builders could have no idea that their small chapel was to become the gathering place of thousands of pilgrims over the future centuries; that here was the future Shrine of Notre-Dame du Cap.

It had been the sad sight of Pierre Boucher's broken-down church that had moved Monsignor de Saint Vallier to appeal to the generosity of the faithful on both sides of the St. Lawrence river, asking them to work on "the construction of a new church", pointing out that he had "promised an abundant contribution towards the fabric", expressing the conviction that the new church would soon rise from the ground "if the habitants on both sides of the river will contribute - and we do so exhort them for the honour of the great Saint, their patron, and for their own advantage."

In 1854, the year of the proclamation of the dogma of the Immaculate Conception, a Cap de la Madeleine parishioner, Zéphirin Dorval, gifted his parish church and, more specifically, the altar of the Brotherhood of the Rosary, with a statue of Mary. It depicts the Virgin as delicate-featured, eyes lowered, and she is standing in the attitude of the Virgin of the Miraculous Medallion, as revealed to the clairvoyant Catherine Labouré in Paris, in 1830. The statue was placed on the altar of the chapel's one and only transept, which became the "chapel of the Rosary", used by the parishioners to address their prayers to Mary.

That holy man, the Vicar of Ars once said: "Leave a parish for twenty years without a priest and when you come back the villagers will be worshipping animals." When their priest, Father Vachon, died in 1729, the parish of Cap de la Madeleine did, in its own way, experience the truth of Saint Jean-Marie Vianney's words. For over a century, this Christian community was deprived of a parish priest. A number of the habitants moved to Montréal. It was, in reality, a miniature exodus, a splitting up of the parish family. Cap de la Madeleine, never a large community, was reduced to a handful of settlers. It was once more a way-station, served occasionally by the passing missionary.

The grassroots work of Father Vachon faded from memory; the former votaries of the Brotherhood of the Rosary turned to other occupations; only tenacity could resist the ebb-tide of faith. The tiny parish of Sainte Marie Madeleine was to live the words of Christ: "A grain of wheat remains no more than a single grain unless it is dropped into the ground and dies. If it does die, then it produces many grains."

"Hail to you, full of grace, the Lord is with you!
Our Lady of the Cape, you open your arms to welcome your children! Great and small, you listen to and comfort everyone; you show them Jesus...
I pray to you for those who are ill, tired or discouraged. Grant them relief from their pain and the ability to offer it with Christ. May we be attentive to their sorrows and their needs."

Pope John-Paul II

Former secretary of Monsignor Cooke, Luc Desilets was appointed priest of the parish of Sainte Marie Madeleine du Cap. The parish, at the time, had a population of about a thousand and was reputed to be hard to handle. "The new priest's pastoral instruction was severe and reformative, yet his parishioners were to remember him as a charitable, pious and dedicated man, particularly devoted in the care of the sick." (Dictionnaire biographique du Canada).

He was an enterprising man, actively involved in political life, and was a regular contributor to the local newspaper, the Journal des Trois-Rivières, which he and his brothers bought in 1872.

In 1885, Monsignor Laflèche appointed him vicar-general of the diocese. On August 30, 1888, at the relatively young age of 56, this fervent votary of the Marian devotion died of a heart attack.

The first statue of Saint Joseph and the Infant Jesus. It was placed above the side altar of the Shrine, following the transfer of the statue of the Virgin to the high altar. It remained there till 1904.

"Remember for ever what you owe to the intercession of Our Lady of the Holy Rosary and Saint Joseph and offer up your heartfelt thanks both to them and through them to Our Saviour."

Luc Désilets

Je me souviens

I shall not forget

1717 : Laying of the cornerstone of the Shrine, June 17.
1718 : The French national symbol - the Gallic-cock is installed.
1719 : Setting up of the lilied cross.
1755 : Deportation of the Acadians.
1759 : Anglo-French war for the control of Canada.
1762 : Issuing of decree for the building of the sacristy on 12 September. Completed in 1764.
1763 : The Treaty of Paris, by whose terms New France was ceded to Great Britain.
1776 : Independence of the United States of America.
1789 : The French revolution.
1791 : The territory of the Laurentides is divided into Upper and Lower Canada.
1830 : Appearances of Our Lady of the Miraculous Medallion to Catherine Labouré.
1837 : Uprising of the Patriots.
1841 : Arrival of the first Oblates in Montréal.
1852 : Foundation of the diocese of Trois-Rivières by Monsignor Cooke, on June 8.
1854 : Beginning of the construction of the cathedral of Trois-Rivières. Completed in 1858.
1858 : Appearances at Lourdes to Bernadette Soubirous.
1867 : Canadian Confederation.
1870 : The first Vatican Council during the pontificate of Pius IX.

Amongst contemporaries of this time were the musicians Bach, Vivaldi, Handel, Haydn, Mozart.

"Is this not
a clear sign
of heavenly intervention?'

The task of the new priest, Luc Désilets, was to arouse the languid faith of his parishioners, who had been without a parish priest for more than a century. When he arrived, the population of Cap de la Madeleine was about one thousand strong.

One day, something strange attracted Father Désilets' attention. He was returning from the vestry, where he had been to hear confessions, and stopped for a moment to pray. It was the eve of the Feast of the Ascension, 1867, but the church was empty. Suddenly, the priest was astonished to see a pig with a rosary between its teeth. The thought came to him unbidden: "The rosary falls from men's hands to be picked up by the swine." It was subsequent to this curious incident that Father Désilets decided to propagate the devotion to the Rosary and he dedicated himself to Our Lady of the Rosary on November 5, 1867.

Gradually, enthusiasm began to awaken and drowsy faith shook off its lethargy. The Brotherhood of the Rosary enjoyed renewed popularity and the tiny 1714 church which could barely hold a congregation of 60, became too small for the parish. People began to talk of a new church, the third in the history of the parish. Unfortunately, money was a very rare commodity; as for building stone, it was only to be found on the opposite side of the St. Lawrence river. Nonetheless, the project of a new church was approved by the churchwardens in the Fall of 1878. The stone was hewed and dressed on the South shore, ready to be carted over the frozen river once winter set in. But the winter of 1878-79 was temperate... and the parish could not afford the luxury of having the stone ferried across the waters.

"By the end of November, 1878, the priest was asking his parishioners to pray for a bridge of ice over the St. Lawrence, so as to be able to bring over the building stone. I followed his suggestion and every Sunday after High Mass, I went to the side-chapel of the Shrine, to the altar of the Brotherhood of the Most Holy Rosary, and there, at the feet of Our Lady of the Cape, I told my beads..."

L.-E. Duguay

"The rosary falls from men's hands to be picked up by the swine."

Luc Désilets

The testimony of Father Duguay

"On March 14, a high wind broke up the ice blocking the mouths of the Saint-Maurice River and fringing the northern shore of the St. Lawrence. The broken ice drifted downstream into the bay of Cap de la Madeleine, helping to cover over the river to a distance of several hundred feet below the church."

"During mass I announced, on the parish priest's behalf, that there would be a High Mass on the 19th to petition Saint Joseph for a bridge of ice. I added that, after vespers, I would accompany those who desired to prospect a passage to the far shore of the St. Lawrence river."

"When we reached the area where the river was covered, we saw that the drift ice was scattered thinly amongst floating snow... We advanced onto the river, choosing places where the fragments of old ice seemed to be close together. The distance between the broken-up floes varied considerably. On and on we went. Firmin Cadotte led the way, axe in hand, a rope round his waist, held by Flavien Bourassa... just in case!..."

"From stopping place to stopping place, we made our way to the final floe of old ice. It must have been about 1,000 feet from the inshore ice along the southern shore... When I looked up, I saw that my two guides had moved on about 200 feet: they had realized that if they went upriver, diagonally, they might be able to reach the inshore ice which stretched out from the Sainte Angèle strand. Still moving forward, Firmin Cadotte struck through the thin ice with the head of his axe. The other men watched us go on, but did not dare follow, so that, in the end, my two guides and myself were the only ones to reach the South shore..."

"Firmin Cadotte crawled forward, feeling with his hand for a small strip or patch of ice which would take the weight of his knee... Thirty men worked along this 1,600 feet stretch until 11 o'clock that night, with only three lanterns to light them in their task, which was to prepare a track wide enough for two carts to pass each other."

"We came back at 11 p.m. Stopping next to the old sacristy I asked my men: "Well, what's the next step?" Firmin Cadotte answered me: "We have to pour water over the bridge in order to make it thicker." At 3 a.m. the same night, we were back at work on the ice. The night was crisp, considering it was the end of March, and the bridge was already solid enough to walk on."

"On March 18, at 4 a.m., the north wind had blown up and driven the clouds away. We sent off for some men to pour more water over our bridge and to saturate the snow which had fallen during the night. We were beginning to be proud of our bridge. When we tested it with a blow from an axe, we found that it was already six inches thick. This raised everyone's hopes of success."

"We had instructed Joe Bellefeuille and his son to prepare six-foot blocks of stone. While we were deciding where to open up the track (there had been a deal of snow overnight), we saw the first sleigh coming over our bridge. It was driven by Joe Longval who had been eager to bring over the first load of stones."

"The working party, which had begun on Wednesday the 19th, lasted until the following Wednesday evening... By Sunday 175 sleighs had passed... We had transported about a thousand feet of dressed stone, plus stone for the foundations. I ordered a stop to the work, and no one undertook to make another voyage."

"It was quite extraordinary, a real miracle. It defied common sense. We immediately named it the Bridge of the Rosary."

David Dubé, one of the artisans of the bridge of ice

"Is this not a clear sign of heavenly intervention? Can one not manifestly see the finger of God?"

Father Désilets

"...this is, to my mind, a great blessing from Almighty God, through whom the Most Holy Virgin has chosen a plot of land in your modest diocese and has made of it a centre of Marian celebration... indeed, I tell you, the Rosary which has been set up here will become a bulwark of our Faith..."

Father Duguay to Monsignor Laflèche
Nov. 20, 1893

Louis-Eugène Duguay, born at St. Jean Baptiste de Nicolet, on March 4, 1852. He was ordained on August 11, 1878 and appointed assistant-priest to Father Désilets on August 21, 1878, at the age of 26. He succeeded Father Désilets as parish priest in Cap de la Madeleine, a post he held from 1888 to 1902. He was the priest for St. Barnabé-nord from 1904 to 1930. He died on April 19, 1930 at the age of 78.

An interior view of Sainte Marie Madeleine church, blessed on October 3, 1880 by Monsignor Laflèche.

Je me souviens

I shall not forget

1852-1870 : Monsignor Thomas Cooke, first Bishop of Trois-Rivières.
1870-1898 : Monsignor Louis-François Laflèche, second Bishop of Trois-Rivières.
1873-1897 : Teresa of the Infant Jesus.
1876 : Pope Pius IX declares Saint Anne to be patron saint of the civil province of Québec.
1878-1903 : Pontificate of Pope Leon XIII.
1883 : First public pilgrimage to the Shrine of Notre-Dame du Cap, on May 7.
1883-1884 : Pope Leon XIII publishes two encyclical letters regarding the rosary.
1885 : Foundation of the diocese of Nicolet. Hanging of Louis Riel.
1886 : Monsignor Alexandre Taschereau, the first Canadian cardinal, is appointed to Québec.

Contemporaries of this period included the musicians Gounod, Tchaikowsky, Debussy and Ravel; the writers Péguy and Veuillot; the scientists Louis Pasteur and Albert Einstein.

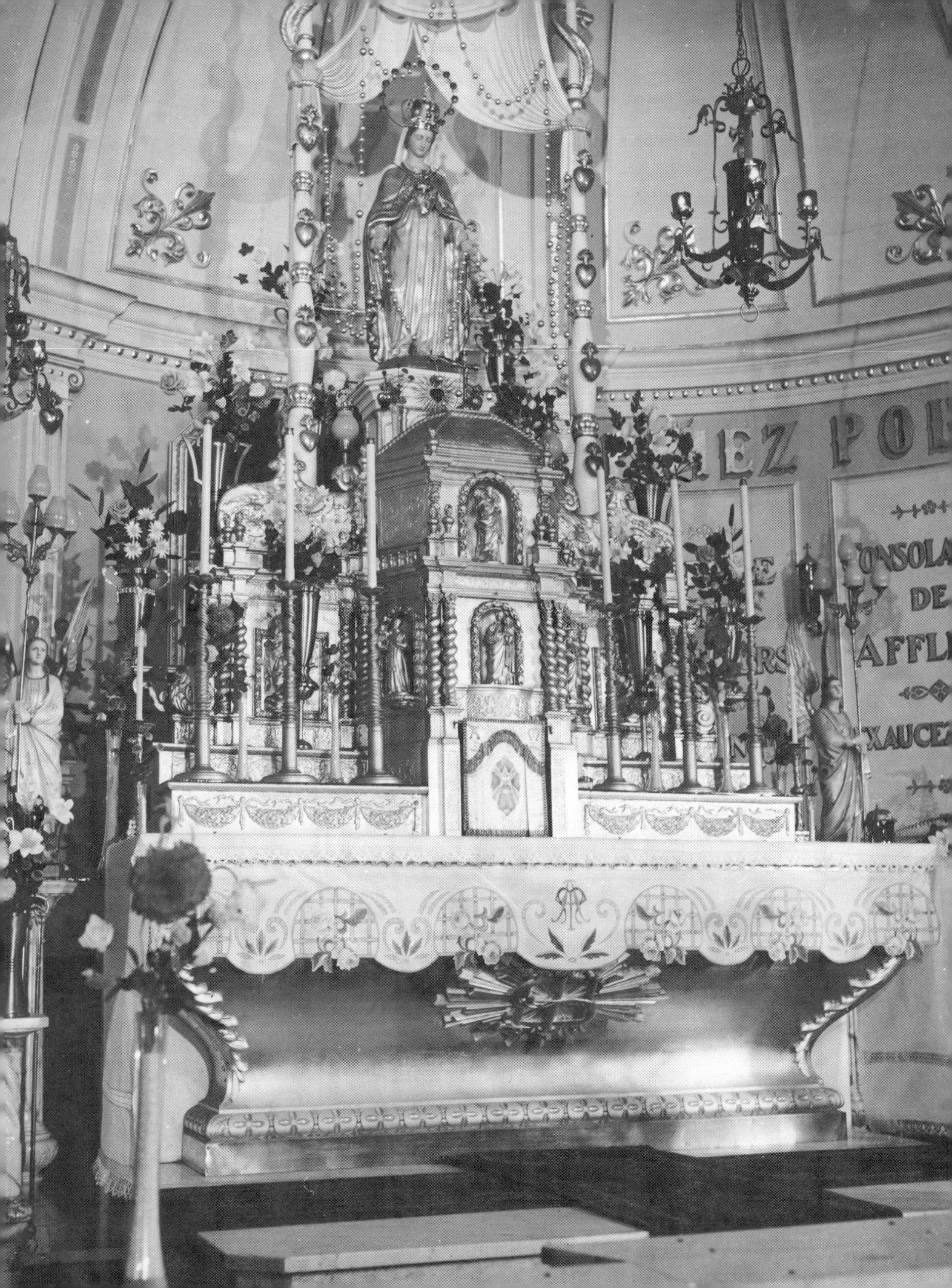
EZ PO
ONSOLA
DE
AFFL
XAUCEZ

"Henceforth
this Shrine
will be dedicated
to Mary"

"Each year, thirty to forty thousand pilgrims visit the modest chapel of Cap de la Madeleine and leave in a state of spiritual and temporal grace under the protection of the Immaculate Virgin."

Monsignor Cloutier, April 20, 1900

At the beginning of March, 1879, Father Désilets had made "a formal vow to the Holy Virgin, the import of which was that if, at this advanced stage of the season, she would grant him a bridge of ice, allowing him to bring over enough stone to build the new church up to the height of the windows, then he would maintain the old church, dedicate it in perpetuity as a place of devotion to the cult of the august Queen of Heaven, the said church to be named Our Lady of the Most Holy Rosary."

The years went by. Ten years passed since the extraordinary creation of the bridge of ice over the St. Lawrence, and the priest had still not kept his promise. But who could blame him? Times were hard, and the available money had gone to the building of the new church. In order to keep his promise he would have to spend money on restoring the old church. And then, Father Désilets could not always be there. He was kept in Rome, along with Monsignor Laflèche, dealing with diocesan problems. Happily, there was Father Frédéric. His providential coming in 1881-82 had led Father Désilets to rely on his support. Our good priest desired that, once the chapel had been solemnly dedicated to Our Lady, there would be someone there to take care of the services, and the welcoming and organization of pilgrimages. "Who better for the task than Father Frédéric," thought he.

Father Désilets who, according to Father Duguay, was known to be a serious-minded person "most ardently desired that heaven should assure him that by dedicating the tiny church to the honour of Mary, he was carrying out the wishes of Our Lady and not indulging his own desires."

"It was on September 29, 1881, that I met the Servant of God for the first time. He arrived from Trois-Rivières by canoe, paddled by the three Désilets brothers, Gédéon, Alfred and Petrus. As I saw him coming up from the water's edge towards Mr. Luc Désilets, who was waiting for him at the end of the promontory, I was struck by his modest expression and unassuming demeanour. Calm, spare of figure, austere, he corresponded to my own image of St. Francis of Assisi..."

L.E. Duguay, at the Beatification proceedings, 1927

But Providence had its own designs. Obliged to return to the Holy Land on May 1, 1882, Father Frédéric later noted "I left Canada on May with regret in my heart, yet mingled with some hope that I should return to that hospitable land, to those simple folk living in the love of God..." Father Désilets was a perspicacious man. He had seen in Father Frédéric a person "used to receiving the Jerusalem pilgrims, a man more than ready to be of assistance."

On June 15, 1888, Father Désilets' hopes were realized and Father Frédéric arrived at Cap de la Madeleine. The old chapel had been restored and, on June 22, it was to be dedicated. The long-awaited ceremony took place in the morning. Father Désilets officiated at the sacrament of the Eucharist. Father Frédéric, freshly arrived from the Holy Land, "was the moving spirit of that unforgettable day", according to Father Duguay, then assistant priest for the parish of Cap de la Madeleine. The Franciscan father had been asked to deliver the sermon marking the occasion, and in it he prophesied the future vocation of the Shrine of Notre-Dame du Cap.

"Henceforth this shrine shall be dedicated to Mary. Pilgrims will come hither from every family in the parish, from every parish in the diocese and from every diocese in Canada. I tell you, that this modest house of God will not suffice to hold the multitude of those who will come to invoke the power and the munificence of the mild Virgin of the Most Holy Rosary."

Father Frédéric

After mass, the statue was taken from the aide altar and placed on the high altar, where it has remained since that day. Henceforth, the ancient parish church of Sainte-Marie-Madeleine was to be the official Shrine of Notre-Dame du Cap. By this gesture, thanks were finally rendered for the extraordinary event of the bridge of ice. At the end of this day of joy and prayer, the pilgrims went their way. Nothing untoward had marked the ceremonies... but the day had not yet drawn to its close.

In the evening, a handicapped man named Pierre Lacroix arrived at the presbytery. The Fathers Désilets and Frédéric conducted him to the Shrine to pray before the statue. It was then that the "prodigy of the eyes" took place.

"The statue of the Virgin had been sculpted with the eyes cast down. Now they were wide open, the gaze fixed. The Virgin was looking straight ahead, Her eyes level. It could hardly be an optical illusion: Her face was clearly visible, illuminated by the sun which, shining through one of the windows, filled the whole Shrine with light. Her eyes were black, well shaped and in perfect harmony with the rest of Her face. The Virgin's expression was that of a living person, at once grave and sad. This marvel lasted somewhere between five and ten minutes."

Father Frédéric, 1897

Our Lady of the Cape
Queen of the Holy Rosary
Open your eyes upon all pilgrims.
We dedicate our lives to you.
Favourite of the Holy Spirit
Obtain a new missionary zeal
That will carry the Church toward
the third millennium of Christianity.

"...I went into the Shrine about seven o'clock in the evening. I was with Father Luc Désilets and Father Frédéric... Well, I was praying and then I took a look at the Holy Virgin, just in front of me. I could see clearly that the statue's eyes were wide open. She looked quite natural, just as if she was staring over our heads...

I didn't say a word, just went on looking at the statue, when Father Désilets got up - he was on my right - and went over to Father Frédéric and I heard him say: "Do you see it?" "Yes," Father Frédéric answered, "the statue has opened its eyes, hasn't it." "Yes it has. But is this really taking place?"

So I said that I'd seen the same thing, been watching it for several minutes, and I'm making this solemn declaration because I believe in my heart and conscience that it is true and I know that this declaration has the same force and binding effect as if it had been made under oath."

Pierre Lacroix, 1895

Those who witnessed the "prodigy of the eyes" saw in it a sign from heaven expressing the wish that pilgrims should be drawn to this Shrine. The news spread like wildfire: that same year, 1,500 pilgrims came to the Shrine on June 24th - a national holiday - and by the end of the year more than 10,000 pilgrims had made their way to Cap de la Madeleine.

Some weeks after this marvel, Father Désilets had said: "This our undertaking is desired by God and required by the Holy Virgin." But the ways of God are not those of men. On August 30 of the same year, the first artisan of the Shrine, Luc Désilets, died suddenly. He was only 56 years old. Serenely confident in the future, he told his successor, Louis-Eugène Duguay: "Father Frédéric will help you. It is no accident of Providence that he is here with us."

"Following the sudden death of Father Luc Désilets on August 30, 1888, Monsignor Laflèche appointed me parish priest and asked Father Frédéric to stay on in Cap de la Madeleine in order to help me deal with parish finances and welcome pilgrims. He worked with me for fourteen years, organizing and serving the pilgrimages, continuing at the same time with his work for the Holy Land... Mine was, perhaps, the hand which executed the instructions, but his was the moving spirit which animated our work. At the celebration dinner in 1915, marking the Golden Jubilee of his entry into the Franciscan order, I told him that our achievement was his alone since nothing had been achieved without him."

Louis-Eugène Duguay, 1927

The first recorded public pilgrimage dates back to May 7, 1883, and started from Trois-Rivières. In 1896, 35,000 pilgrims were reported. Thanks to a quay built on the river itself, visitors came directly to the Shrine by boat.

In 1896, the first trainloads of pilgrims arrived, using a branch line that CP had set up for these pilgrimages.

It was only at the beginning of the twentieth century that pilgrims began to arrive by car, travelling along the "King's Way".

On the far left, the presbytery. To its right, the Shrine and the 1891 extension. On the far right, Sainte-Marie-Madeleine church (1880) and in the foreground a quay under repair.

Je me souviens

I shall not forget

1887	: First pilgrimage by boat.
1891	: First extension to the Shrine. First store for the sale of religious articles.
1892	: Publication of first number of "The Annals of the Most Holy Rosary."
1894	: Development of the spring. The miraculous statue is embellished with a rosary: the beads were a gift from Father Frédéric and were set into a rosary by the Ursulines of Trois-Rivières.
1895	: First recorded candlelight procession. Exhumation of the body of Father Paul Vachon: the skeleton was in a perfect state of conservation.
1896	: Setting up of the first Way of the Cross (terminated in 1900) modelled after that of Jerusalem. First pilgrimage by train, on October 2.
1899-1934	: Monsignor François-Xavier Cloutier, 3rd Bishop of Trois-Rivières.

Father Frédéric Jansoonne, Franciscan

"You have
sent us
a saint"

Frédéric Jansoonne, born in Ghyvelde, France, on the Flemish Belgian frontier, on November 19, 1838. From the age of 16 to 24, he worked as a commercial traveller in the cloth industry. He joined the Franciscans on June 26, 1864, at the age of 25. He was ordained on August 17, 1870. He was then 31. He died in Montréal on August 4, 1916. His mother tongue was Flemish.

"You have sent us a saint; both a saint and a priest of extraordinary power... He is universally sought after... The sick seek him out and follow him everywhere... He is a Man of God... The more one has to do with him, the more one comes to venerate and admire him... If you should see his superiors, you may assure them that he lives like a saint... You have to live with this extraordinary man to really appreciate his virtue, intelligence, warmheartedness and nobility."

Luc Désilets, 1881

"I knew Father Frédéric over a period of 35 years... He was my mentor, my support, my guiding angel in the various undertakings of my sacerdotal career. When, as assistant priest and later parish priest, I faced financial difficulties, dealing with organized pilgrimages, he was providential and helped me to control both the spiritual and temporal aspects of my task, with disinterested skill and kindness.
I do believe he died like a saint... He never claimed to have wrought miracles... He had a childlike trust in the Most Holy Virgin... He used to speak of Her with tears in his eyes. There came a time when his devotion to the Most Holy Virgin took over his whole life and he became the artisan of an estimable and admirable piece of work. I am talking, of course, of the pilgrimages to Cap de la Madeleine... Thanks to him, the word spread of this Shrine that Mary had chosen and marked out with her preference... The Shrine soon became the meeting ground for every kind of physical and moral distress. The sick found healing, the sinners were filled with deep remorse and penitence."

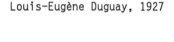

Louis-Eugène Duguay, 1927

At the age of 37, Father Frédéric was a missionary in the Holy Land, where he worked as deputy-assistant to the keeper of the holy places. He put new life into the pilgrimages to the Holy Land, and renewed with the tradition of processing through the streets of Jerusalem, visiting the Stations of the Cross. Here, Father Frédéric can be seen preaching in front of the Holy Sepulchre.

A part of the Way of the Cross, carved in wood. It is modelled on that of Jerusalem and was begun in 1896 and terminated in 1900. The artisan, Mr. Pierre Beaumier, was known as "the carpenter of Notre-Dame du Cap". The work was carried out under the direction of Father Frédéric. The day will come when such wooden constructions will fall victims to the ravages of time.

"The impression he received as the Virgin steadily gazed forth, shall remain stamped before his eyes... Were he an artist he would certainly make a faithful reproduction of what he saw on June 22, 1888." Father Frédéric wrote that text but had it signed by Father Duguay. The Franciscan had too much humility to make a personal declaration on the subject, and it was this text that appeared in the newspaper La Presse in May, 1897.

Fresque on Father Frédéric's tomb, Trois-Rivières.

At the funeral of Father Frédéric on August 7, 1916, the Bishop of Trois-Rivières, Monsignor F.-X. Cloutier, eulogized the departed in the following terms: "It was Father Frédéric who played the major role in the devotional undertaking of Our Lady of the Rosary in Cap de la Madeleine. The man known, justifiably, as "the prophet of Notre-Dame du Cap" carried out an immense task during the fourteen years he worked as director of pilgrimages. Like the saints, he rendered all glory and all praise to God.

> "I work for the glory of Our Lady of the Most Holy Rosary at Cap de la Madeleine. I am in charge of all pilgrimages to the shrine. Yesterday there were pilgrims who had come from far away... The problem is that our people are on the way to spoiling everything... They ask to be cured of all their sicknesses... and that is where they commit their error "toto caelo" (completely). Instead of praying Mary "Salus infirmorum" (Help of the sick), they ask me to cure them, unambiguously and at the top of their voices! I begin to be alarmed... "ô fides" (Oh, Faith!)

Father Frédéric to P.R. Delarbre, O.F.M., 1891

Amongst Father Frédéric's numerous talents was that of being a writer. He wrote a number of books, pamphlets, articles and many letters. There was one publication in particular which, first published in January, 1892, would last till today. This was the Annals of the Most Holy Rosary, which became, in 1919, the Annals of Notre-Dame du Cap and, finally, in 1970, had its name changed to Notre-Dame du Cap Revue. The Annals were originally a response to Father Désilets' desire that there should be "an unpretentious revue detailing the more remarkable of the favors granted to her votaries by the Holy Virgin..." Father Désilets was the principal artisan and promoter of this revue while he worked at the shrine.

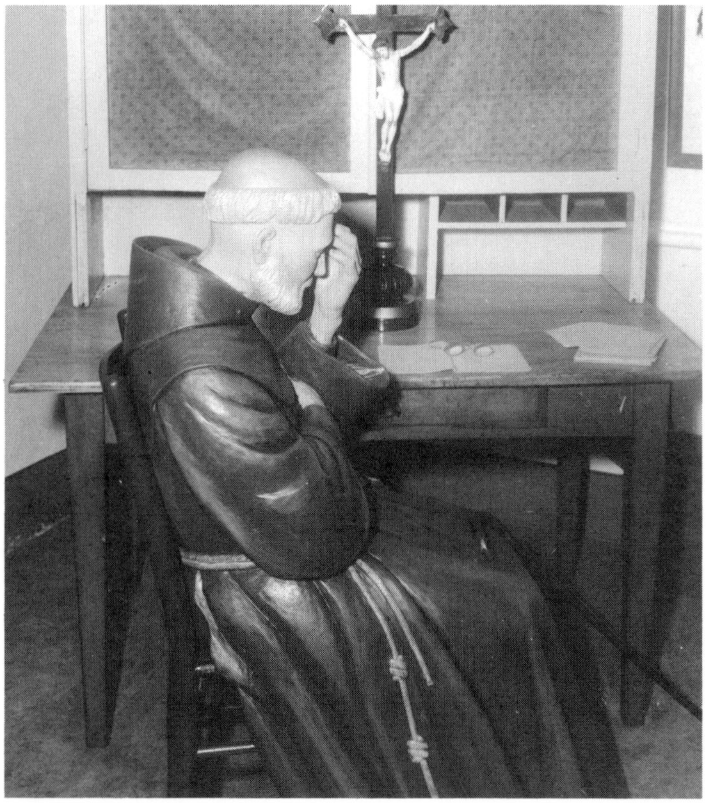

Polychromatic wood sculpture showing the disciple of Saint François at prayer. It illustrates the words of Saint François, who desired that "his brothers, following the tradition of the Apostles, should possess but one garment and nothing else under the sun, so that they might follow as closely as possible Our Lord Jesus Christ, who was born in a stable, always lived in poverty and died on the Cross, stripped of all and totally abandoned."

Letter to his family, July 3, 1865, sent from the novitiate of Amiens, France.

A part of the crypt at Trois-Rivières where the remains of Father Frédéric are entombed. It was opened in September, 1938. The tomb itself was opened in 1948 and 1988 : it was seen that his body was mummified.

Je me souviens

I shall not forget

1876 : Father Frédéric received his assignment for the Holy Land on May 4. He was 37.

1881 : He received his authorization for Canada on July 14.
He remained at the presbytery of Cap de la Madeleine from September 29, 1881 to May 1, 1882.

1888 : Father Frédéric returned to Cap de la Madeleine on June 15.

1890 : The Franciscans opened a house in Montréal, followed in 1900 by one in Québec and, in 1903, one in Trois-Rivières.

1898 : The English-speaking Franciscan tertiaries in Montréal made a gift of a crown and a heart for the miraculous statue.

"Specifically
entrusted
with their
Mother's interests"

"We recognize that this is not an undertaking whose existence depends merely on the zeal or the talents of the individual. There have been difficulties in the past, there have been obstacles. The undertaking has flourished in spite of this; it is made to endure."

Monsignor F.-X. Cloutier, 1902

The Bridge of the Rosaries, inaugurated on August 15, 1924, in memory of the bridge of ice over the St. Lawrence river.

"I congratulate and encourage the Oblate Missionaries of Mary Immaculate, who have been in charge of this Shrine for the past 82 years... The ministry of Notre-Dame is also a missionary charge. It must contribute to the renewal of the people of God. And it corresponds to the mainstream of your Marian spirituality which you have helped reinforce and spread throughout Canada."

John-Paul II, 10 September, 1984

The unexpected death of Father Désilets was a blow to the future of the Shrine and a heavy burden for the priests. But, as the departed sometimes would say, "God is never short of resources." The future, like the past, had to tread the path of trust in God's projects. It is no easy task to kill off something that God believes in!...

> "For a moment, we were afraid that the great enterprise of the pilgrimages was nothing more than the result of one man's devotion, called upon to disappear when he passed on, as happens when a work is linked too closely with personal initiative. But no, these trials bore the stamp of God, the imprimatur of an imperishable undertaking."

Monsignor L.-F. Laflèche

Father Duguay, remarking that more and more pilgrims were coming to the Shrine, became an ardent believer in the development of the pilgrimages. But, quite understandably, he began to find the work too much for his slender resources. Father Frédéric and himself could no longer cope with the numbers of pilgrims who came from all parts. When the pilgrimage season began, he had to call on numerous priests from neighbouring religious communities to lend a hand. Father Duguay, in many ways a true St. John the Baptist, came straight out with his problem on November 20, 1893, when he said:

> "In spite of all the links which bind me to you, in spite of the fact that my life is completely bound up with this parish, I must step down... and leave the place to a religious order."

A Montréal daily, describing the intense activity at the Shrine, following the arrival of the Oblates, wrote: "As late as yesterday, opposite the old shrine, there was a gulley, an 80-foot wide ravine, 350 foot long and 20 feet deep. Today it is filled in, and there is no trace of the former ravine... the teeming energy of life is at work."

The presbytery as it was when the Oblates arrived in 1902.

"I am presently at Cap de la Madeleine, on a mission... the presbytery, where I have my room and where I keep all the documents of the Commissariat, is perched on the edge of the huge, majestic St. Lawrence river, which, covered in haze, resembles a glowing furnace! This is one of the most beautiful natural sites in the area."

Father Frédéric

The founder of the Oblates of Mary Immaculate, the blessed Eugène de Mazenod, had accepted, on behalf of his sons, the charge of several places of pilgrimage in France. He saw these Marian shrines as their "home mission". This ministry, which had appealed so specifically to Monsignor de Mazenod, inspired the Bishop of Trois-Rivières who, in 1926, declared:

> "When I decided to put the Shrine's organization on a permanent basis, I asked myself which religious order I would do best to invite here. So I consulted Father Frédéric and, after reflecting for a few minutes, he replied: "Invite the Oblates of Mary Immaculate."

After considerable negotiation and consultation, Monsignor Cloutier asked the Oblates to take in hand the Shrine of Notre-Dame du Cap.

> "Nothing could be more suitable than that the true sons of Mary should be specifically entrusted with their Mother's interests... They are more particularly charged with taking care of the poor."

After serious consideration, the Oblates accepted the charge. On May 7, 1902, the first senior priests arrived to take over the Shrine. Father Duguay bid farewell to his parishioners on May 8, 1902. As for Father Frédéric, he continued to preach in the area and to accompany pilgrims to Notre-Dame du Cap.

> "Thanks to the Oblates, the undertaking grew: it was a mighty tree and its kindly branches spread not only over Canada but stretched out to our neighbours in the United States of America..."
>
> Monsignor Cloutier, February 17, 1926

In virtue of a decree issued by Pope Pius X, Monsignor Cloutier crowned the miraculous statue on October 12, 1904. The celebration took place in a huge marquee in front of the Shrine. There were 15,000 people in attendance. Father Frédéric was carrying the crown. He was ecstatic, the dream of his life was about to come true. He exclaimed, "Now, at last, I can sing my 'Nunc Dimittis'." The crown was stolen during the night of June 20-21, 1981.

On the left, the marquee in front of the Shrine, ready for the crowning of October 12, 1904. There was room for only part of the crowd to enter. In the centre, Sainte-Marie-Madeleine church. On the right, the 1904 extension.

The store for the sale of religious articles, in 1910. On the right, part of the kiosk of the Annals of the Most Holy Rosary.

When the Oblates arrived in Cap de la Madeleine, the parish had a population of 300 families. It was a poor parish, scattered along about 10 miles. There was only one road. A contemporary pilgrim wrote: "I myself took part in two evening pilgrimages, in 1897. I saw the speaking poverty of the place, from the quayside to the parish church we were lighted by a few, sparse, oil-soaked brands. The parish church itself was candellit by huge chandeliers hanging from the vaulted ceiling. Inside, there were about 1,000 pilgrims filling every nook and cranny of the church which, poor and shabby as it was, resembled much more a barn than house of God."

F.-X. Pelletier, O.M.I.

In 1909, the Fathers of the Plenary Council of Québec expressed the following wish: "It is desirable that the faithful of Canada make a pious pilgrimage to Cap de la Madeleine, where a Brotherhood of the Rosary has been in existence for over 200 years, and where a statue of the blessed Virgin Mary, crowned by His Holiness Pope Pius X, is the object of solemn demonstrations of faith and piety."

A candlelight procession round lake Sainte-Marie.

"Such pilgrimages allow us to enjoy what some have called "Hours of heaven", in the joy of the Faith, with Mary. And far from being an escape from our daily routines, this experience imbues us with new strength to live the Gospel in today's world."

John-Paul II, 10 September, 1984

The first Station of the Rosary in the Gardens of the Virgin. Our Lady accompanied by St. Dominique, on her left, and St. Catherine of Sienna, on her right.

Je me souviens

I shall not forget

1903-1914 : Pontificate of Saint Pius X.
1903-1904 : Construction of the Oblates' residence and of a new extension to the Shrine. Arrival of the Little Sisters of the Holy Family.
1906-1908 : Planting of some 800 trees.
1906-1910 : Stations of the Rosary in the Gardens of the Virgin.
1913-1916 : A new Way of the Cross and the stone tomb.
1914 : First World War and the Spanish flu.
1914-1922 : Pontificate of Pope Benoît XV.
1915 : Golden Jubilee of Father Frédéric's admission into the Franciscan order on July 22.
1916 : The Rock of the Calvary and the Grotto of the Pieta. Death of Father Frédéric on August 4.
1917 : Appearances of the Virgin at Fatima.
1921 : Mackenzie King, Prime Minister of Canada.
1922-1939 : Pontificate of Pope Pius XI.
1925 : Beatification of the Canadian martyrs. Canonization of Teresa of Lisieux.
1926-1944 : Monsignor Odilon Comtois, 4th Bishop of Trois-Rivières.
1927 : Arrival of the Soeurs Servantes de Jésus-Marie, a contemplative order of nuns which prays for the work of the Shrine. Initiation of beatification proceedings and the study of all the texts written by Father Frédéric.
1937 : Construction of the House of the Pilgrim, which began as a retreat. Reconstruction of the tomb in dressed stone.
1938 : Lake Sainte-Marie, the kiosk, the Rock of the Virgin.
1939-1945 : Second World War.
1939-1958 : Pontificate of Pope Pius XII.

Beauty fair

Humble Maiden, Beauty fair
Queen of Heaven, our pride and joy
Humble Maiden, Beauty fair
Blessed Mother of God

Come into the Garden
To the Tree of Life
Come into the Garden
In the Kingdom of God

Mary, you are Mother
Of the rich and poor
Mary, your are Mother
In the Kingdom of God

Kind and gentle Lady
Shining light of hope
Kind and gentle Lady
In the Kingdom of God

A. Dumont

ST-
NARCISSE

ave maria
S. ROSAIRE
PRIEZ POUR
NOUS
MON ESPRIT
EN DIEU
MON SAUVEUR
SUR SON
HUMBLE
SERVANTE
GÉNÉRATIONS
ME DIRONT
EST SON
NOM
EN AGE

Bishop de Laval, during a pastoral tour, navigating the St. Lawrence River, accompanied by a Frenchman and an Amerindian.

The parable of the Good Samaritan: "There was once a man who was going down from Jerusalem to Jericho..."

In front of the ramparts of Quebec City, Samuel de Champlain waving the fleurs-de-lis banner; in his right hand the City Charter.
Armorial bearings of the Province of Quebec.

The parable of the father and the two sons: "Father, give me my share of the property now."

Stained glass windows by Jan Tillemans, O.M.I.

Pilgrims at the spring.

Gathering of young people for the Feast of the Assumption, 1975.

Stream fed by lake Sainte-Marie.

By lake Sainte-Marie.

▲ The Basilica viewed from the South Shore of the St. Lawrence River.

▲ Pilgrims at the stations of the Rosary.

▲ Pilgrims at the Marian celebration by lake Sainte-Marie.

▲ Celebration for sick people, August 15.

▲ The Bridge of the Rosaries.

▲ Pilgrims in front of the tomb.

Stained glass window by Jan Tillemans, O.M.I. The family Rosary. ▼

◀ Stained glass window by Jan Tillemans, O.M.I. Notre-Dame du Cap, Queen of the Holy Rosary.

TOUTES

Mother, at your feet is kneeling

Mother at your feet is kneeling
One who loves you is your child
Who has sighed so often to see you
Bless me, Mother, bless your child
Mother, when my Jesus calls me
From this world so dark and drear
From the wily snares of Satan
Shield me, Mother, Mother dear

Dearest Mother, tell my Jesus
How I love him fond and true
And oh Mary, dearest Mother
Tell him I belong to you

Plead for me when Jesus judges
Answer for me when he asks
How I spent so many moments
How I performed so many tasks
Mary, oh my dearest Mother
May it ever to me be given
As on earth I fondly love thee
So to love thee still in heaven

Sister S.C. (old hymn)

"From coast
to coast"

In 1947, the tide of fervour for Marian devotion took the statue of the Madonna over the whole country. For seven years, the statue travelled extensively, from Halifax to Vancouver.

Following the long and sombre period of two World Wars, there was a revival of Marian fervour. The Marian Congress, held in Ottawa in 1947, gave rise to this post-war movement of Marian piety. To mark the occasion, a replica of the miraculous statue was brought to Ottawa, making numerous halts along the way in the parishes which lined its itinerary. The pilgrim statue was displayed during the ten days of the Congress. Close to half a million believers came to pray to Notre-Dame du Cap. There are mentions of numerous healings and conversions during this period.

In 1954, Pope Pius XII decreed a Marian year. The Oblates of the Shrine suggested a coast-to-coast tour of the statue of Notre-Dame du Cap, as a fitting preparation for the Marian Congress to be held in Cap de la Madeleine from the 5th to the 15th of August, 1954. Placed on a float reminiscent of the Bridge of the Rosaries, Notre-Dame du Cap made her own pilgrimage - 4,300 miles across Canada and the United States of America.

> "It is not easy to assess the spiritual value of such a tour. But if one's yardstick is the millions of Hail Marys recited day and night before the Madonna, the hundreds of thousands of dedications to the Immaculate Heart of Mary which were renewed at Her feet and, above all, the incalculable number of confessions and communions to which Her coming gave rise, then one cannot but affirm that She made a truly triumphal voyage... The Oblates sang the glories of Mary in the churches, in the streets, everywhere. And everywhere they went they strove to bring people to the knowledge and love of Mary and to stretch Her reign from coast to coast."
>
> Report of the Marian Congress, 1954

View of the temporary altar at the Marian Congress, Ottawa, 1947.

Notre-Dame being welcomed by the crowds. This typical scene was repeated from coast to coast.

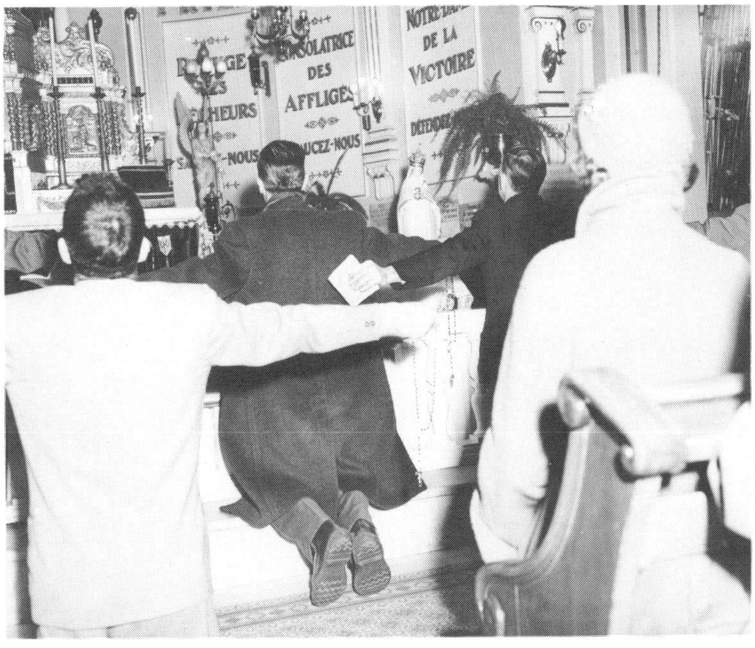

Inauguration of the Perpetual Rosary at the Shrine on May 1, 1953, in anticipation of the Marian Congress planned for Notre-Dame du Cap during the Marian Year of 1954.

These French-speaking groups have been known since then as the "Rosary groups". Each year some 50,000 pilgrims return to gather at the feet of Notre-Dame du Cap. Organized groups of english-speaking pilgrims count for some 25,000 of those who come to pray Our Lady of the Rosary each year. If one could number all the Hail Marys which have risen from this Shrine since its inauguration, they would certainly form an immense bridge of rosaries, spanning the generations and stretching from coast to coast...

During the Marian year of 1954, pilgrims flocked to the Shrine of Notre-Dame du Cap from every part of Canada and of the United States of America. Two jubilees were celebrated in that same year: the hundredth anniversary of the dogma of the Immaculate Conception and the golden jubilee of the crowning of the miraculous statue. They were an outburst of popular celebrations of the Faith: from August 5 to August 15, the Coliseum of Trois-Rivières hosted 15 performances of a spectacular presentation, "Our Lady spreads her cloak from coast to coast"; and thousands of pilgrims attended an exhibition of the history of the Marian devotion in Canada, held on the site of the Shrine.

August 15, 1954, marked the climax of the Marian celebration. To preface the ceremony of the second crowning of Notre-Dame du Cap, on the Exhibition grounds in Trois-Rivières, an immense Marian parade had been organized: 21 allegorical floats illustrated local or national Marian events; the procession was accompanied by close to fifty parish escort units and 15 brass bands from the four corners of Québec and Ontario. An immense crowd of visitors from all over the country came to pay homage to Notre-Dame du Cap on the occasion of this second crowning, presided over by the Papal Legate, Cardinal Valerio Valeri.

> "Never in living memory has Trois-Rivières seen such a huge demonstration. The Marian parade was the most grandiose, the most spectacular, the most brilliant and the most evocative event ever to take place in our city..."
>
> Le Nouvelliste, 16 August, 1954

Our Lady of the Cape
You are the every-day mother.
You are the one who entered our lives
And whose presence we always feel.
You are the one to whom we can speak freely
without preparing our words.
The one to whom we like to pray
when we need rest.
The one we know is untiringly disposed to answer our needs.

The crown placed on her head represents the Canadian people's homage to the Madonna. Because of its great value, the crown was not left permanently on the head of the celebrated statue, but was brought out only on important occasions. Otherwise, she wore the 1904 crown. The 1954 crown was stolen during the night of August 15-16, 1975.

From year to year, the Gardens of the Virgin are made more beautiful, creating a more prayerful atmosphere. "...our great-nephews, as they make their way round the Stations of the Cross, will not, perhaps, realize that we planted long rows of elms here in the spring of 1908... this site used to be a huge ravine, and it took close to 200,000 loads of earth or sand to fill it in." A comment that we find in the Annals published early in the century, underlines the importance of nature as a meeting ground for man and God. Our predecessors' remark bears out the belief that we have shared over the generations: "Our dream is to beautify in every possible way, to improve unceasingly... If we are mistaken, then Mary too is in error, for it is She who is guilty of infusing Her pilgrims with so much piety and enthusiasm!"

The Annals, 1905-1909

In the background, the House of the Pilgrim, facing lake Sainte-Marie.

A celebration for the sick in the Gardens of the Virgin, circa 1955.

Je me souviens

I shall not forget

1946-1947	:	Monsignor Maurice Roy, 5th Bishop of Trois-Rivières.
1947-1975	:	Monsignor Georges-Léon Pelletier, 6th Bishop of Trois-Rivières.
1948	:	Louis Saint-Laurent, Prime Minister of Canada. The cause of Father Frédéric is advanced thanks to a miracle obtained through his intercession, in Japan.
1949	:	Shifting of the residence of the Oblates, August.
1950	:	The campaign for the Family Rosary.
1953	:	Blessing of the new church of Sainte-Marie-Madeleine by Monsignor Pelletier, July 12.
1958-1963	:	Pontificate of Pope John XXIII.
1960	:	The Quiet Revolution in Québec. The building of the House of the Madonna.
1963	:	Opening of the Ecumenical Council, Vatican II. Demolition of the Sainte-Madeleine Oratory (the 1880 church). Lester B. Pearson, Prime Minister of Canada.
1967	:	Expo 1967, Montréal. Centenary of the Canadian Confederation.

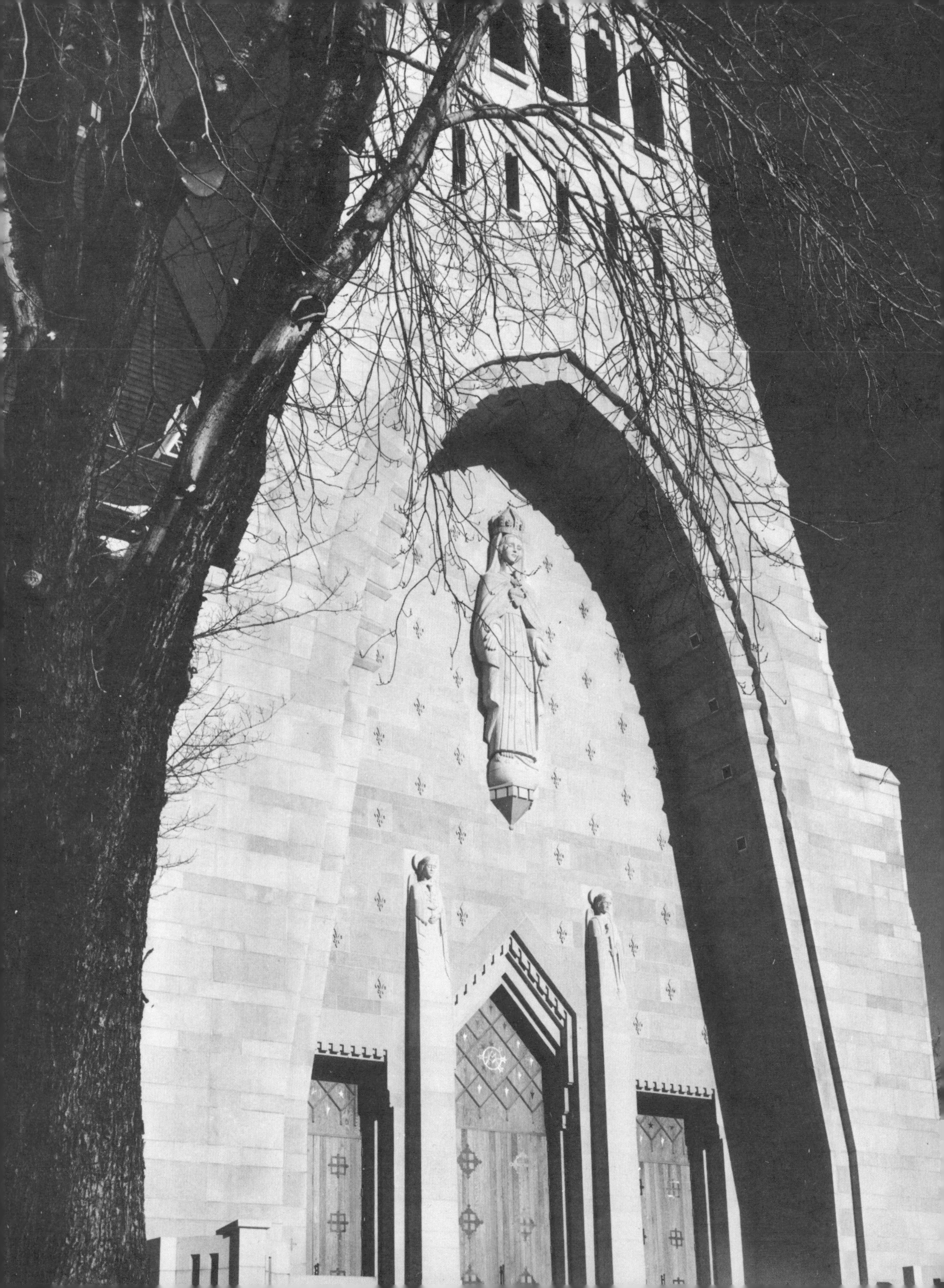

"The wind
blows where it
wishes"

The Basilica in the evening, during a candlelight procession following the preaching of the novena of the Assumption.

"This temple is the expression of the Faith of a people... It was the poor who paid for the Basilica. It was born of the Bridge of Rosaries. It was created through the piety of our people."

Paul-Henri Barabé, O.M.I.

On their arrival in 1902, the Oblates were already saying "We dream of a majestic temple raised to the glory of the Holy Virgin." In 1913, they began a campaign, through the Annals of Notre-Dame du Cap and encouraged by Monsignor Cloutier. The project for the construction of the Basilica was finally launched in 1937. But it was a project which was to take time to realize.

> "The Canadian episcopate joins with the Bishop of Trois-Rivières in enjoining the swift realization of the project as outlined and assures those generous benefactors who help towards its completion of their blessings."
>
> The Canadian Episcopate, June 22, 1939

But with the advent of the Second World War this great dream was to be put aside for the duration. It was only in the summer of 1949 that the project finally began to take shape. The residence of the Oblates was shifted, in order to clear the site of the future Marian temple. On August 5, 1955, the first spadeful of earth was turned and the excavations officially commenced. The building of the Basilica was placed under the protection of the artisan Saint Joseph, whose statue remained on the building site throughout the period of construction.

In August, 1957, the cornerstone was placed and blessed. On August 14, 1964, the Basilica was consecrated by Monsignor Georges-Léon Pelletier, Bishop of Trois-Rivières. On the following day, the Feast of the Assumption, the solemn inauguration was held.

> "This temple of imposing proportions and majestic lines was not, and could not be, the mere outcome of human planning. Faith is stronger than the projects of nature, as God is stronger than mortal man. May the sublime Queen of the Most Holy Rosary cherish us eternally in Her heart and instil in us He who is the Way, the Truth and Life."
>
> Monsignor G.-L. Pelletier, 1964

In 1973, a new annexe replaced that of 1904. The stones on the right-hand wall come from the 1879 Bridge of Ice.

Opening in October, 1962, and closing in December, 1965, the Vatican II Council raised a great many questions about the Church and its role. Pilgrimages and Marian devotion were amongst the subjects dealt with. A new world was in the making; an old world was about to take its leave. The Shrine of Notre-Dame du Cap had its own crisis to face, its own pilgrimage to accomplish.

One of the most authoritative spokesmen of the time, Father Paul-Henri Barabé, when interviewed in 1979, said: "Once the Basilica had been inaugurated, many people sat back comfortably, saying, 'Now we're all set to go...' But the wind was changing, bringing with it a new climate, the climate of the modern world. And all this came about under the influence of the shock waves of change rippling out from Vatican II." Father Noël Poisson, then director of pilgrimages, had this to say: "After the high point of the years leading up to 1964, there was a slump. There is no denying that interest fell off. The Rosary groups dropped to almost half their number. It was a period of decline."

But the Holy Spirit had not abandoned the Church, nor yet this place of pilgrimage. The prayer that Pope John XXIII requested as an offering for the forthcoming Ecumenical Council soon fulfilled itself beyond all possible expectations. In those years, Christians often had this prayer on their lips: "Renew in our time the Pentecostal marvels."

The liturgical renewal which resulted from Vatican II breathed new life into the Shrine. A new creative life, which touched both hymns and music. It was in the spring of 1968 that "rhythmic masses" were introduced in the basement of the Basilica. They brought with them a breath of creativity, of adaptation, of faith which honoured the spirit of the Vatican II Council, anxious to see the liturgy evolve into a participatory activity. For 25 years, the choir has contributed to the post-Vatican II liturgy. Everything in the Basilica is designed to encourage prayer and meditation: the stained-glass windows, opening to the heavens and evoking our history and a world invisible to our eyes, the magnificent creation of the Dutch Oblate, Jan Tillemans; the Casavant organ, whose harmonies swell and fill the very vaults of this Marian temple. This corresponds to the spirit of Vatican II, which expressed the hope that the art of our time, of our peoples and of our world might flourish untrammeled, providing it paid due respect and honour to the temple and to the holy rites of the Church.

The organ was built in St. Hyacinthe and has 75 stops and 5,544 pipes, distributed among three keyboards and the pedal board.

Little by little, the inspiration of Vatican II modified the approach to preaching, which returned to its biblical sources, while adopting modern mass-communication techniques. In this post-Council context, the Novena of the Assumption was radically modified. Henceforth, the preaching of this highlight of the Shrine's pastoral was entrusted to a team of some ten persons. Those in charge were the first to feel the beneficial effects of the spiritual springtime which the Church of the Seventies was to experience. They were defining the 'home mission' for the contemporary world.

The Shrine opens its doors to the mass media. Studio R.M. expands from broadcasting the Rosary over the local radio station to becoming a recording studio for the production of religious songs and music. R.M. Editions diversifies its production: a team of producers open up the Québec market, offering diaporamas which deal with the most sensitive areas of the post-Vatican II pastoral and catechism. Radio programs are designed and produced at Studio R.M. and broadcast over all Québec. The novena of the Assumption is broadcast first on radio and later on television.

A group of young people gathered for an evening of charismatic prayer in 1975.

When a wave of spiritual renewal reached Québec in 1973, the Shrine of Notre-Dame du Cap was there to welcome it. "Charismatic renewal" created a new interest in spontaneous prayer and marked an increase in the number of pilgrims coming to the Shrine. Bible study groups were created to satisfy the desire for the Word of God. Thanks to regular attendance, these classes ran for several years.

To celebrate the centennial of the Bridge of Rosaries, the Shrine offered a week of perpetual rosaries. Between March 18 and March 25, 1979, thousands of people came to pray to Our Lady, the spiritual founder of Notre-Dame du Cap. On the 22-23 March, the Shrine welcomed the pilgrimage of the Oblates of Eastern Canada, presided over by their Superior General, Father Fernand Jetté. After the sacrament of the Eucharist had been celebrated, under the direction of Monsignor Laurent Noël, Bishop of Trois-Rivières, a commemorative plaque was unveiled and set up on the stone wall in the Shrine extension.

> "Everywhere, we strive to build bridges, bridges between men. Between the whites and blacks in South Africa; between Buddhists and Christians in Asia; between the rich and the poor throughout the world. But we must also build bridges between God and Man, so that we may save a Church which is made not of stone but of living souls, and which will be the true Church of Jesus Christ."

Fernand Jetté, O.M.I., 1979

A group of Oblates of Eastern Canada accomplishing their pilgrimage on the occasion of the centennial of the Bridge of Ice, March 1979.

Je me souviens

I shall not forget

1956-1964 : Manufacture of the Basilica's 350 stained-glass windows.
1963-1978 : Pontificate of Pope Paul VI.
1968 : Pierre-Elliot Trudeau, Prime Minister of Canada.
1973 : New extension to the Shrine.
1974 : New Stations on the Way of the Cross, a gift from the parishioners of Saint Célestin.
1975 : Monsignor Laurent Noël, 7th Bishop of Trois-Rivières.
1976 : The Parti Québécois took office.
1978 : Pontificate of Pope John-Paul I, August 26-September 28.
: Pontificate of Pope John-Paul II, elected October 16.
1980 : Death of master-glassmaker Jan Tillemans, O.M.I.

"A shower of grace"

PRIEZ POUR
TOUTES LES
GENERATIONS
LE PUISSANT

On September 10, 1984, Pope John-Paul II made a pilgrimage to Notre-Dame du Cap. The successor of St. Peter had arrived in Quebec City the day before, and this was now the second day of his pastoral visit of Canada, scheduled to last from September 9 to September 20.

> "It is my dearest wish that I may make a pilgrimage to the major Marian sanctuary of each country I visit. I am, thus, moved and overjoyed to become one of Mary's pilgrims in this Her Shrine and to recommend to Her, our Mother, my apostolic mission and the fidelity of all Christians in Canada."
>
> John-Paul II, 10 September, 1984

The great gathering to welcome the Pope began with the angelus prayer, to the sound of the bells from the old shrine. The hearts and souls of the crowd had been prepared for this celebration of the Faith by songs, prayers and exhortations.

The Pope arrived at about 4 o'clock. His first action was to enter the 1714 shrine, where he knelt down. After addressing the guests, John-Paul II toured the site in his popemobile before going to the podium, from which he was to preside over the sacrament of the Eucharist.

Pope John-Paul II delivering the homely after the gospel of the MAGNIFICAT.

Gathered together under the theme "Let us celebrate our Faith", a crowd of 75,000 pilgrims defied the rain which fell all through the Pope's day of pilgrimage.

"My brothers and sisters, I must congratulate you on this celebration. I must also congratulate you on your hardiness... hardiness in the face of the rain! But if I am to congratulate you on your hardiness, I must also congratulate you on the rain!... In the Old Testament, rain always had a symbolic value; it symbolised grace. Rain is the symbol of grace. And it is with this key that I wish to unlock the mystery of our celebration of the Faith. I believe that this celebration of the Faith in the house of our Mother has a profound resonance because of the sacrifice that accompanied our prayers. For all these reasons, I must congratulate you. And I do so with all my heart. I believe also that the strength of the singing during the celebration has strengthened our Faith..."

"These moments of pilgrimage are highlights in the life of a Christian, exceptional moments of communal and private prayer, touched with a freedom and liberty that is not always possible to find at home. These occasions allow one to recharge one's Faith through listening to the Word of God. We come here to lay our cares and our requests at Mary's feet, with an unquestioning confidence that is precious to God. At the same time, it often happens that we rediscover our own Christian, sacerdotal or religious vocation. The contemplation of Mary Immaculate leads us to quests for purification and the sacrament of repentance. We feel the need to renew our hearts, to fill them with the Holy Spirit. I am certain that many of you after praying here with Mary, as the disciples did during Pentecost, will leave with increased apostolic fervour."

John-Paul II at the Shrine, 10 September, 1984

"Virgin of Cap de la Madeleine, you open your arms to welcome your children! Young and old, you listen to them, console them and bring them to the knowledge of the source of all joy, all peace: Jesus, the fruit of your womb."

John-Paul II, 10 September, 1984

Pope John-Paul II greets the crowd for the last time, accompanied by Monsignor Laurent Noël, Bishop of Trois-Rivières.

"Many thanks! I greet you. And I greet with you the Virgin whom you venerate in this Shrine. I am happy to have been able to join with you in this act of veneration. Farewell!"

John-Paul II, 10 September, 1984

Following the pilgrimage of Pope John-Paul II to the Shrine of Notre-Dame du Cap, the favours of Our Lord and of Mary were renewed day after day. The henceforth celebrated day of September 10, 1984, marked the beginning of a new, increased fervour, pride and interest in visiting the Shrine.

The Feast of the Pentecost on June 7, 1987, began the Marian year, which ends on August 15, 1988. On the evening of the 6th, John-Paul II presided over the prayer of the Rosary in the basilica of Santa Maria Maggiore in Rome. Notre-Dame du Cap was one of thirteen Marian shrines chosen to relay the television broadcast of this religious event throughout the world. This opening ceremony of the Marian year filled the Basilica of Notre-Dame du Cap to capacity.

On the same evening, a crowd of 2,000 gathered in the basement of the Basilica to hear a recital of Marian chants and a lecture on Mary, given by a biblical specialist. The candlelight procession began at 11 p.m., followed by midnight mass, presided over by Monsignor Martin Veillette, assistant Bishop of Trois-Rivières. The whole night was devoted to uninterrupted prayer as group succeeded group in the Shrine.

On Pentecost day itself, the primate of the Canadian Church, Cardinal Louis-Albert Vachon, presided over the Eucharistic service in the open air, in the presence of a number of bishops and a congregation of several thousands. The miraculous statue had been carried in procession to the site of the celebration. It was the first time Notre-Dame du Cap had been taken out of the Shrine since the 1954 Marian year. The day ended with the launching of the book "The Lord is with Thee".

June 7, 1987: the opening of the Marian year. Open-air celebration of the sacrament of the Eucharist presided over by Cardinal Louis-Albert Vachon.

Television relay of the Rosary, presided over by Pope John-Paul II in the Basilica, June 6, 1987.

Je me souviens

I shall not forget

1978 : The theologians agreed on the heroic nature of Father Frédéric's virtues.
1980 : Referendum in Québec.
1983 : Jubilee of the Redemption proclaimed by John-Paul II.
New parking on land formerly belonging to Consolidated Bathurst.
1984 : Brian Mulroney, Prime Minister of Canada.
1985 : On March 18, John-Paul II declared Father Frédéric to be "Venerable".
1987 : Two committees of doctors agreed that Father Frédéric performed a miracle in Japan.
Monsignor Martin Veillette appointed auxiliary Bishop for Trois-Rivières.
Death of Mr. René Levesque.
Encyclical letter "The Mother of the Redeemer" by John-Paul II.
1988 : 150th anniversary of the birth of Father Frédéric, November 19.
Centenary of Notre-Dame du Cap
Beatification of Father Frédéric, Rome, Sept. 25

"Look around you

and see..."

Our generation has not forgotten... the past with its favours and miracles. A past which is still in our hearts and which illuminates our present.

United as one family, we share in the pilgrimage of Faith. We tread the same paths as those who have gone before us.

There have always been pilgrimages. Whether the weather is fine or foul, whether there is a crisis of faith or a renewal, in the present as in the past, the pilgrims still come.

When one sees what God has done in this place of pilgrimage from one generation to another, one can but echo the psalm: "You have made many wonderful plans for us; I could never speak of them all - their number is so great!

Nature is not only designed for poets! It is not a source of inspiration reserved to artists and mystics! The pilgrim drinks deep of nature, quenching his thirst as he drinks in God. This is true of all men and women, both poor and rich, both sick and healthy.

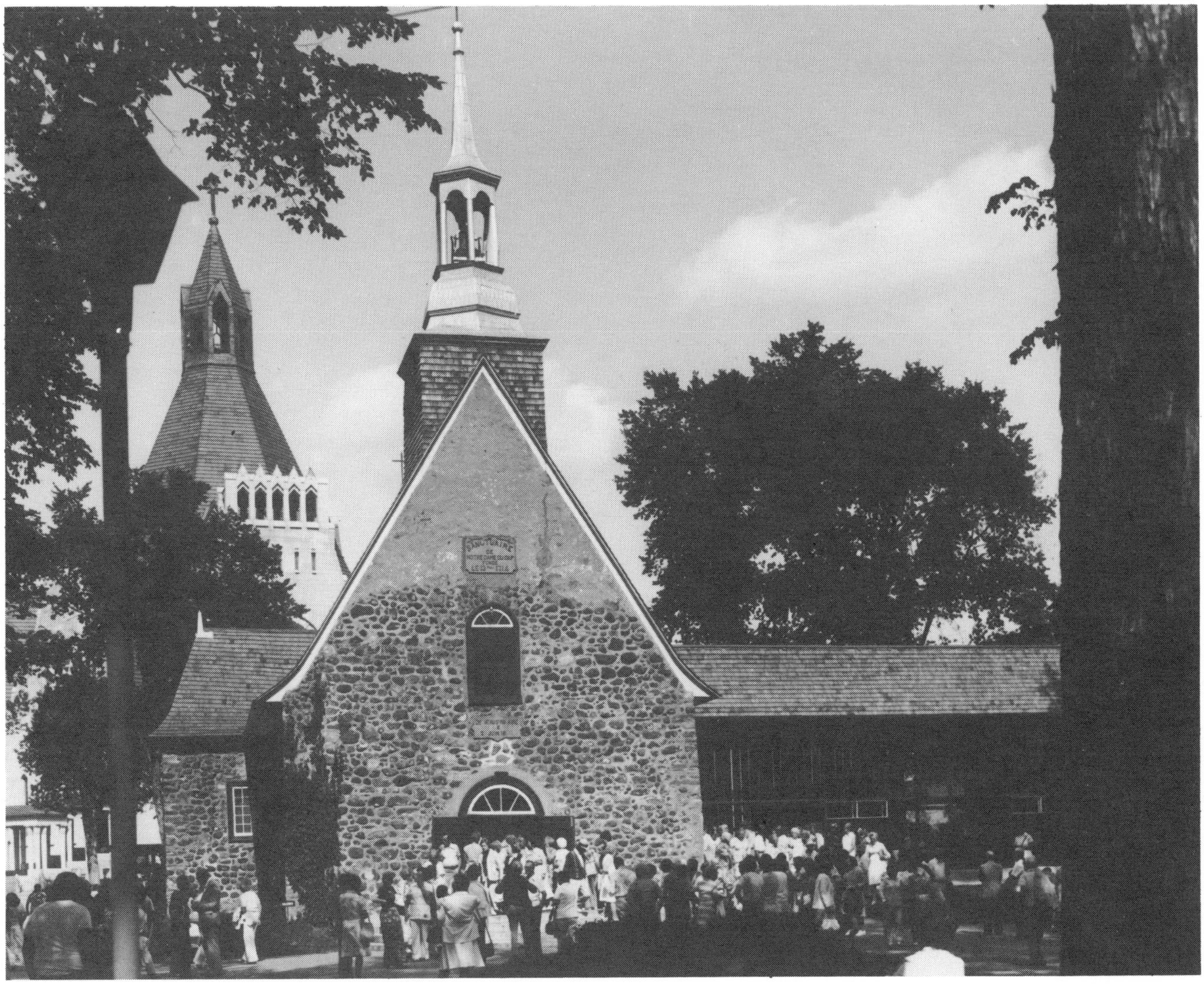

"I was glad when they said to me, 'Let us go to the Lord's house.' And now we are here... where the tribes come... to give thanks to the Lord..."

Psalm 122

"Tomorrow's flowers are contained in today's seeds."

Chinese proverb

"This Marian pilgrimage is an immense grace accorded to the Canadian people. May the river of the prayerful never run dry here."

John-Paul II, 10 September, 1984

"The Holy Virgin is responsible for everything here..." These words, spoken by the unassuming priest, Father Duguay, were true when they were uttered at the end of the 19th century, and remain as true at the end of our present century.

"Magnificat!"

Pilgrims of fleeting time, we shall not forget... We shall not forget those who first carried the Gospel into this small corner of our country, those first citizens, pioneers, builders: untiring workers whose hearts responded to the same challenge - to raise a temple for a Christian people and its Mother.

Pilgrims of fleeting time, we shall not forget... We shall not forget the artisans of the Bridge of Ice, the pastors, their numberless helpers. Our hearts send up our infinite thanks to all those past benefactors of Notre-Dame du Cap.

Pilgrims of fleeting time, we shall not forget... We shall not forget the sublimity and magnificence of our Lord's actions here, accomplished through the intercession of Our Lady of the Holy Rosary. At the dawn of this third millenary, we bear witness for future generations. And from generation to generation the same summons will ring out, gathering us together to celebrate the roots of our past.

> We shall not forget "things we have heard and known, things our fathers told us. We will not keep them from our children; we will tell the next generation about the Lord's power and his great deeds and the wonderful things he has done." (Psalm 78)

Pilgrims of fleeting time, we shall not forget...

Paul Arsenault, O.M.I.

Contributors

Photographs

NDC Collection except:
Roméo Flageol: 107-110
Paul Hamel: 90, 119
Arturo Mari: 104, 105
Jérôme Martineau: 116, 124
Normandin Photographes: 7, 11, 15, 24, 57, 112, 113, 123

Colour photo section:

NDC Collection except:
A. Mari: 14, 15
J. Martineau: 6, 11, 12, 13
Normandin Photographes: 2, 4, 5, 10
Saint-Cyr Photo: 14

Archives

André Boucher, O.M.I.

Technical Advisors

Fernand Savard, O.M.I.
André Dumont, O.M.I.

English translation

Geoffrey Vitale, Ph.D.
Associate professor, UQTR
on behalf of
TRADUCTIONS DE VILLERS-CÔTÉ INC.
Trois-Rivières

Table of Contents

Graphic design: Gralicom Inc., Thetford Mines, Québec
Printed by l'Imprimerie l'Éclaireur, Beauceville, Québec
April 1988